Contents

Contents

Introduction

The interaction between freedom of speech and various legal concepts shapes how expression is limited in democratic societies. Freedom of speech, a crucial human right, allows people to share opinions and question authority. Yet, this freedom faces legal complexities that aim to balance open expression with protecting values like individual reputations, national security, and legal proceedings' integrity.

In this context, concepts like defamation, contempt of court, political libel, and tort law become relevant, prompting discussions about where to set the boundary between unrestricted speech and responsible communication.

By looking into significant cases such as *Tisdall, Ponting,* and *Daniel Ellsberg and the Pentagon Papers*, we can understand how the connection between free speech and legal limits has changed over time. This exploration will look into the details of these legal concepts and the careful balance they aim to strike. By observing how society deals with the tensions between individual expression and community interests, we gain a better understanding of the ongoing effort to protect free speech while maintaining essential democratic principles and justice.

Freedom of Speech

Freedom of speech is a crucial human right in democratic societies, protecting individual freedoms. It includes the right to express thoughts, opinions, beliefs, and ideas without fear of censorship or punishment. This right is recognised in various international declarations, like the *Universal Declaration of Human Rights*, and in the United Kingdom (UK), it is enshrined in the *Human Rights Act 1998, Article 10.*

At its core, freedom of speech encourages open dialogue and diverse perspectives. It allows citizens to express dissent, question authority, and engage in public discourse. By facilitating the free exchange of information and ideas, it supports informed decision-making and accountability, acting as a check against government overreach and abuse of power.

While freedom of speech is important, it has limits. Speech that encourages violence, promotes hatred, or spreads false information can be harmful and disrupt social harmony. Societies aim to balance protecting free expression and preventing harm, and these limits depend on cultural, legal, and societal norms.

In modern times, digital platforms, especially the internet, have changed how we think about free speech. While it allows for extensive expression, it brings challenges like online harassment, misinformation, and the role of big tech companies in content regulation. Finding a balance between preserving free expression and controlling harmful content is a ongoing challenge.

Freedom of speech is not just a legal principle; it is a cornerstone of vibrant democracies. It empowers marginalised voices, promotes innovation, and encourages creative exploration. The ability to openly critique governments, institutions, and societal norms fosters growth and progress. However, the right to freedom of speech should not be used as a shield for hate speech, discrimination, or incitement to violence. Responsible exercise of this right demands respect for the rights and dignity of others. It involves engaging in constructive conversations that lead to understanding, empathy, and positive change.

In conclusion, freedom of speech is a multifaceted right that underpins democratic societies. It enables the expression of diverse viewpoints, drives social progress, and holds those in power accountable. While limitations exist to prevent harm, the responsibility to exercise this right thoughtfully and ethically rests with each individual. Striking a balance between preserving free expression and protecting against harm is essential for maintaining a just and equitable society.

Official Secrecy

Official secrecy refers to the practice of withholding certain information or documents from public access in order to protect national security, sensitive government operations, or confidential information. It is a concept prevalent in many governments worldwide, aiming to strike a balance between transparency and the need to safeguard critical interests.

Governments often classify information as "secret," "confidential," or "top secret" based on its potential impact if disclosed. Such classification is crucial for ensuring the security of a nation, preventing unauthorised access to sensitive data, and safeguarding diplomatic, military, or intelligence operations. Official secrecy is particularly vital in areas involving defence, national strategy, foreign relations, and critical infrastructure.

However, the implementation of official secrecy has raised concerns about transparency, accountability, and citizens' right to access information. Striking the right balance between national security and public accountability is a complex task. Transparency is essential for maintaining trust in government actions and decisions, as well as for holding authorities accountable for their actions. In democratic societies, legislations like the *Freedom of Information Act 2000* and oversight by independent bodies help ensure that official secrecy is not abused to suppress information that should be accessible to the public. These mechanisms facilitate responsible disclosure of certain classified information while respecting legitimate security concerns.

Nonetheless, official secrecy remains a contentious issue. Overclassification can hinder public discourse, impede investigative journalism, and limit citizens' ability to engage in informed debates about government actions. Balancing the need for secrecy with the principles of openness, democracy, and public interest requires continuous review and fine-tuning of policies.

In conclusion, official secrecy serves as a necessary tool for safeguarding national security and preserving sensitive government operations. While its implementation is essential, it should be accompanied by mechanisms that ensure transparency, accountability, and citizens' right to access information that does not compromise security. Striking this balance is crucial for upholding democratic values and maintaining public trust in government institutions.

The Interplay

The relationship between freedom of speech and official secrecy is complex. On one hand, freedom of speech demands transparency and the availability of information to the public. Without access to essential information, citizens cannot make informed decisions or hold authorities accountable. The ability to engage in public discourse is limited when crucial information is kept hidden under the guise of official secrecy.

On the other hand, official secrecy is sometimes required to protect sensitive information that, if disclosed, could jeopardise national security or diplomatic relations. This can create a tension between the right to know and the need to safeguard critical interests. Striking the right balance is challenging, as openness can enhance accountability but also expose vulnerabilities that adversaries might exploit.

Legal mechanisms and frameworks attempt to reconcile these tensions. Freedom of Information Acts and oversight bodies aim to ensure that official secrecy is used responsibly and that citizens have access to information that is not overly sensitive. These mechanisms promote transparency while respecting legitimate security concerns.

In conclusion, the connection between freedom of speech and official secrecy reflects the intricate interplay between the need for transparency and the imperative to protect national security. A democratic society strives to strike a balance where citizens can freely express themselves while understanding the necessity of certain information being kept confidential. Balancing these principles is essential to uphold both individual rights and the nation's security interests.

The Tisdall and Ponting Cases

The Tisdall and Ponting cases are two notable legal episodes in the UK involving issues of official secrecy and the release of classified information. These cases highlight the tensions between government efforts to maintain confidentiality and the public's right to know.

1. **Tisdall Case:** The Tisdall case refers to the legal proceedings involving Sarah Tisdall, a former civil servant in the UK's Foreign and Commonwealth Office. In 1983, Tisdall leaked classified documents to *The Guardian* newspaper, revealing information about government decisions related to cruise missiles. The leaked documents raised questions about the government's foreign policy decisions. Tisdall's actions led to her arrest and subsequent prosecution under the *Official Secrets Act 1920*. She was sentenced to six months in prison for her role in leaking the documents. The case raised debates about the tension between the government's desire to protect sensitive information and the public's right to be informed about matters of national significance.

2. **Ponting Case:** The Ponting case involves Clive Ponting, a civil servant in the Ministry of Defence. In 1984, Ponting leaked classified documents to *The Guardian* concerning the sinking of the Argentine cruiser General Belgrano during the Falklands War. The leaked information contradicted the government's official account of the incident. Ponting's actions led to his arrest and trial under the *Official Secrets Act 1920*. During the trial, he argued that his actions were motivated by a belief that the public had a right to know the truth about the incident. The jury ultimately acquitted Ponting, and the case underscored the importance of whistleblowing and the role of the jury in deciding matters of public interest and national security.

The cases of *Tisdall and Ponting* have brought to the forefront the complex and nuanced relationship between freedom of speech and official secrecy. These legal episodes have sparked discussions, legal debates, and public discourse on how to strike a balance between the public's right to information and the government's responsibility to protect sensitive data.

3. Conflict Between Whistleblowing and Secrecy:

Both cases involve individuals who, driven by their moral convictions, leaked classified information they believed the public should know. Sarah Tisdall and Clive Ponting acted as whistleblowers, revealing government decisions and actions that raised questions about accountability and transparency. Their actions exemplify the tension between the government's efforts to maintain official secrecy and individuals' desire to expose information in the public interest.

4. **Defining Public Interest:** The *Tisdall and Ponting cases* have prompted discussions about how to define the "public interest" in terms of revealing classified information. The cases challenge societies to consider whether certain information, although classified, should be made accessible to the public if it sheds light on government actions that might be contrary to the public's well-being or democratic values.

5. **Impact on Freedom of the Press:** These cases have also raised important considerations regarding the role of the press in acting as a check on government power. Journalists play a crucial role in disseminating information that holds authorities accountable. The *Tisdall and Ponting cases* underscore the role of investigative journalism in challenging official secrecy and contributing to informed public discourse.

6. Legal Protections for Whistleblowers: The *Tisdall and Ponting cases* have influenced discussions about the legal protections afforded to whistleblowers. They raise questions about whether individuals who disclose classified information should be granted immunity from prosecution if they act in the public interest. These cases have encouraged conversations about revisiting laws that criminalise disclosures that expose potential government wrongdoing.

7. Balancing Transparency and National Security: The cases highlight the delicate balance governments must strike between ensuring transparency and protecting national security. While transparency is crucial for democratic governance, governments argue that certain classified information, if disclosed, could compromise national security or diplomatic relations. These cases force societies to grapple with the challenge of finding the appropriate balance between openness and security.

In essence, the *Tisdall and Ponting cases* have cast a spotlight on the intricate interplay between freedom of speech and official secrecy. They have prompted societies to consider the rights of individuals to express themselves, the importance of government transparency, and the potential consequences of exposing classified information. These cases remain pivotal in shaping ongoing discussions about the boundaries of free speech, accountability, and the role of information in democratic societies.

Daniel Ellsberg and the Pentagon Papers

There are similar cases in the United States (US) that parallel the themes of the *Tisdall and Ponting cases*. One notable example is the case of *Daniel Ellsberg and the Pentagon Papers*.

Daniel Ellsberg and the Pentagon Papers: In the early 1970s, Daniel Ellsberg, a former military analyst, leaked a classified government study known as the Pentagon Papers to *The New York Times* and other newspapers. The Pentagon Papers documented the history of US involvement in Vietnam and contained information that revealed government deception about the war's true nature and progression.

Like Tisdall and Ponting, Ellsberg faced legal consequences for his actions. He was charged with theft, conspiracy, and violations of the *Espionage Act*. His trial became a landmark case that raised questions about the tension between government secrecy and the public's right to know about government actions that affect their lives. The case ultimately led to significant discussions about freedom of the press and the role of whistleblowers in exposing government misconduct.

Ellsberg's case also contributed to the ongoing legal debates about whether the government can restrict the publication of classified information on the grounds of national security. The Supreme Court's decision in the *Pentagon Papers case* reaffirmed the importance of press freedom and set a precedent for the protection of publications based on leaked classified documents.

In many ways, the *Ellsberg case* in the US mirrors the *Tisdall and Ponting cases* in the UK, as all three involve individuals who leaked classified information to the press in an effort to expose government actions and challenge official secrecy. These cases collectively highlight the global tension between government transparency, individual conscience, and the public's right to access critical information.

The Official Secrets Act 1989

While the *Official Secrets Act 1989* was introduced in the UK after the cases of Sarah Tisdall and Clive Ponting, it was not a direct response to these specific cases. Instead, the act represents a broader effort to update and modernise existing legislation related to official secrecy.

The Official Secrets Act 1989 replaced previous versions of the Official Secrets Act, including the *Official Secrets Act 1911* and the *Official Secrets Act 1920*. These older acts were deemed outdated and in need of revision to reflect changes in society, technology, and the evolving challenges of maintaining national security while respecting individual rights.

The cases of Tisdall and Ponting, along with other instances of classified information leaks and discussions about government transparency, likely influenced the context in which the *Official Secrets Act 1989* was drafted and debated. These cases brought attention to the tensions between official secrecy, freedom of speech, and government accountability.

Blasphemy

Blasphemy at English common law refers to the offence of speaking or expressing disrespectful or irreverent sentiments towards religious beliefs or deities. Historically, blasphemy laws aimed to protect the religious sensibilities of the majority and maintain social order by punishing those who challenged or criticised established religious doctrines.

In English common law, blasphemy was considered a criminal offence, and individuals found guilty of committing blasphemy could face severe penalties, including imprisonment, fines, or even death. The legal definition of blasphemy often depended on the specific religious beliefs that were dominant in the society at the time.

Over the years, the enforcement of blasphemy laws in England evolved, and there were notable cases that attracted public attention and debate. These cases often raised questions about the limits of freedom of expression, religious tolerance, and the role of the state in regulating speech.

In more recent times, there has been a shift away from enforcing strict blasphemy laws in many Western countries, including England. With the advancement of principles such as freedom of speech and religious pluralism, many legal systems have reconsidered or repealed blasphemy laws to ensure that individuals have the right to criticise or question religious beliefs without fear of legal repercussions.

In the UK, the *Criminal Justice and Immigration Act 2008* effectively abolished the common law offence of blasphemy, replacing it with a more specific offence related to incitement to religious hatred. This change reflected a broader societal shift towards protecting freedom of expression while also recognising the importance of respecting diverse religious beliefs.

Overall, the concept of blasphemy at English common law illustrates the historical tension between religious orthodoxy, freedom of expression, and the evolving legal and social norms that shape how societies approach issues of faith, speech, and religious tolerance.

Contempt of Court

The relationship between contempt of court and freedom of speech is complex and often involves a delicate balance between two fundamental principles: maintaining the integrity of the judicial process and safeguarding the right to express oneself freely. (*Contempt of Court Act 1981*)

1. **Conflict of Interests:** Contempt of court involves restricting speech that could potentially interfere with the administration of justice. It aims to prevent actions that may prejudice ongoing trials, obstruct court proceedings, or hinder the impartiality of jurors. In cases where public discussions, media coverage, or statements made by individuals could influence the outcome of a trial, courts may impose restrictions to preserve the fairness of the proceedings.

2. **Protection of Due Process:** Freedom of speech is a cornerstone of democratic societies, ensuring that individuals can express their opinions, participate in public discourse, and hold authorities accountable. However, in the context of legal proceedings, the exercise of free speech must be balanced against the need to protect the right to a fair trial and the due process of law. Unrestrained public commentary can lead to biased juries, compromised witnesses, or tainted evidence.

3. **Legal Restrictions:** Courts may issue gag orders or reporting restrictions to prevent the media and individuals from publishing or discussing certain details of ongoing cases. These restrictions aim to prevent the dissemination of information that could sway public opinion, unduly influence potential jurors, or undermine the fairness of the trial. While these restrictions may seem to curtail freedom of speech, they are considered necessary to protect the integrity of the legal process.

4. **Public Interest Considerations:** In some cases, the public's right to know and engage in discussions about matters of public interest might conflict with contempt of court principles. Striking the right balance requires careful consideration of the potential impact of public discourse on ongoing legal proceedings.

Overall, the relationship between contempt of court and freedom of speech is a complex interplay of rights and responsibilities. While freedom of speech is a crucial democratic value, it is not absolute and may be subject to limitations when it clashes with other important societal values, such as ensuring a fair trial and upholding the rule of law. Courts strive to find an equilibrium that protects both the right to express oneself and the fair administration of justice.

Political libel

Political libel refers to false statements made about political figures or entities that damage their reputation, often through written or printed publications. The relationship between political libel and free speech raises important questions about the boundaries of expression in the context of political discourse and the balance between protecting reputations and upholding the principles of free expression.

1. **Free Speech Protections:** As discussed, free speech is a foundational principle in democratic societies, allowing individuals to express their opinions, engage in public debate, and criticise government officials and policies. Robust political discourse is essential for informed citizenry and holding those in power accountable.

2. **Public Figures and the Public Interest:** In the context of political libel, public figures such as politicians, government officials, and prominent public figures often have to tolerate a higher degree of criticism and scrutiny due to their role in public life. The legal standard for proving political libel against public figures is typically more demanding than for private individuals. To succeed in a defamation lawsuit, public figures often need to prove "actual malice," meaning the statement was made with knowledge of its falsity or with reckless disregard for the truth.

3. **Protection of Reputations:** While free speech is crucial, there are limits to the protection it provides when false statements harm a person's reputation unjustly. Political libel cases often involve a delicate balance between protecting free expression and safeguarding an individual's or entity's reputation from false and damaging claims. These claims can potentially harm not only the reputation of the targeted figure but also the public's perception of political processes and institutions.

4. **Chilling Effect and Self-Censorship:** The threat of legal action for political libel can have a chilling effect on public discourse. Concerns about lawsuits might discourage individuals from expressing their opinions or criticising political figures. This self-censorship could hinder the vibrant exchange of ideas that is crucial for a healthy democratic society.

5. **Public Interest Defence:** Some jurisdictions recognise a "public interest defence," allowing individuals to defend themselves against defamation claims by arguing that their statements were made in the interest of informing the public about matters of importance. This defence aims to strike a balance between protecting reputations and ensuring open and informed political discourse.

Tort Law and Free Speech

British tort law and free speech intersect in cases where the exercise of free speech may potentially lead to legal claims for defamation, invasion of privacy, or other civil wrongs. While free speech is a fundamental principle, it is not an absolute right and must be balanced with the protection of individual rights and reputations under tort law.

1. Defamation:

Defamation (*The Defamation Act 2013*) is a significant area where free speech and tort law intersect. Defamation occurs when false statements harm a person's reputation. While individuals have the right to express their opinions and engage in open discussions, making false statements that damage someone's reputation without a valid defence can lead to a defamation claim. To strike a balance, British law recognises certain defences like truth, fair comment, and qualified privilege, which allow for free expression while providing remedies for unjust harm to reputation.

2. Qualified Privilege:

Qualified privilege is a defence that allows individuals to make defamatory statements without liability under certain circumstances, such as when making statements in a legislative or public meeting. However, the privilege can be lost if the statement is made with malice or goes beyond what is necessary for public interest.

3. **Freedom of the Press:**

The intersection of free speech and tort law is particularly pronounced in cases involving the media. While the press plays a crucial role in informing the public and holding power to account, it must also be mindful of the potential harm caused by inaccurate or defamatory reporting. English law provides some protection for responsible journalism under the *Reynolds defence*, which shields media outlets from defamation claims if they can show that they acted responsibly in publishing the information.

4. **Invasion of Privacy:**

Privacy is another area where free speech and tort law intersect. English law recognises the tort of invasion of privacy, which addresses the unauthorised disclosure of private information. Balancing the right to privacy with free speech can be challenging, especially in cases involving public interest or information that exposes wrongdoing.

5. **Balancing Rights:**

British courts strive to strike a balance between protecting free speech and safeguarding individual rights under tort law. They consider factors such as the importance of the information, the harm caused, and the potential public interest when determining the outcome of cases involving defamation, invasion of privacy, and related tort claims.

In summary, English tort law and free speech intersect in cases where the exercise of free expression may lead to legal claims for defamation, invasion of privacy, or other civil wrongs. Balancing these rights requires careful consideration of the public interest, individual reputation, responsible journalism, and the broader principles of democratic discourse.

Conclusion

In conclusion, the relationship between free speech and various legal concepts, such as defamation, contempt of court, political libel, and tort law, is a dynamic interplay that reflects the complexities of balancing individual freedoms with societal interests. While free speech is a fundamental cornerstone of democratic societies, it is not an absolute right and often needs to be weighed against other values, such as protecting reputations, preserving fair trials, ensuring government transparency, and upholding the rule of law. Throughout history, landmark cases like *Tisdall*, *Ponting*, and *Ellsberg* have highlighted the intricate tensions between free speech and official secrecy. These cases underscore the importance of allowing individuals to express dissenting opinions and expose potential wrongdoing, while also recognising the need to safeguard national security, diplomatic relations, and the proper functioning of the judicial system.

The legal principles surrounding freedom of speech and related concepts are continuously evolving as societies grapple with new challenges posed by technology, changing social norms, and global interconnectedness. Striking the right balance between individual rights and collective responsibilities requires ongoing reflection, legal adaptation, and respectful dialogue. Ultimately, fostering a society that values both robust public discourse and the protection of core democratic principles remains a nuanced endeavour that demands thoughtful consideration of various perspectives and interests.

Cases

R v Tisdall, [1999] 3 All ER 1025 (CA).
R v Ponting, [1984] Crim LR 317 (CA).
New York Times Co v United States, 403 U.S. 713 (1971).

Legislation

Contempt of Court Act 1981, c 49 (UK).

Criminal Justice and Immigration Act 2008, c 4 (UK).

Defamation Act 2013, c 26 (UK).

Freedom of Information Act 2000. c. 36 (UK).

Human Rights Act 1998, c 42, art. 10 (UK).

Official Secrets Act 1911, c 28 (UK).

Official Secrets Act 1920, c 75 (UK).

Official Secrets Act 1989, c 6 (UK).

Universal Declaration of Human Rights. (1948). Preamble and Articles 1-30. Retrieved from https://www.un.org/en/universal-declaration-human-rights/index.html

Notes

www.ingramcontent.com/pod-product-compliance
Lightning Source LLC
Chambersburg PA
CBHW050755290526
45792CB00008B/2195